CU00840349

Sport Is A Business and Business Is A Sport

Derek Redmond

TABLE OF CONTENTS

THE GUY WHO NEVER GIVES UP

If you have heard of me before, you may have heard me referred to as "the guy who never gives up." You might have seen the video of my 400m semi-final race at the 1992 Barcelona Olympics. You might have seen it on YouTube, heard the story, or even seen it live on TV.

It's quite a tale. It was painful. It was a huge disappointment. And it was a big turning point in my life. And I chose to learn from it.

Now I'm 52 years old. I got a lot from my career as an international athlete. I'm incredibly fortunate to have an amazing wife and four wonderful children. I am privileged to have spent many years pursuing several different sports. Most people know me as a two-time Olympian in both the 400m individual and the 4 x 400m relay. But I was also a professional basketball player in the UK, even representing my country. And I played rugby at both professional and semi-professional levels too.

I'm enormously proud of what I did. It took a great deal of time and dedication. But the simple truth is you don't achieve anything in life without, every once in a while, something coming along and making you want to give up.

There are those times in life when we're lying on the track, so to speak, injured again, and cursing at everyone and everything that's happening.

That's the time when we're faced with life's greatest challenges. That's when we make the biggest decisions. And often our best decisions. Those are the moments when we can choose never to give up.

SPORT AND BUSINESS

I'm thankful to have been involved in all those different sports and to have represented my country. But, beyond the direct sporting knowledge and my actual involvement, I gained some far deeper insights.

There are things I've learnt and things that I now love sharing with others to help them improve their personal lives and to enhance the way they go about their work and their business.

There are two quotes I always love to share with people.

The first one is *"Sport is a business and business is a sport. There's no difference between the two, apart from the activity that you're taking part in."* The second? *"The mindset of a successful businessperson is no different from the mindset of a successful sportsperson."*

The skills and traits it takes to be a world-class sportsperson are exactly the same as those you need to be an accomplished businessperson. To succeed in either arena, you need discipline, perseverance and a real work ethic.

You also need to be able to see that life doesn't pose us problems - it simply gives us challenges. We then have the opportunity to take on and learn to overcome them. Because we simply won't achieve success without being challenged along the way.

There is another saying about there only being two guarantees in life: death and taxes. Well, personally, I think there are three - death, taxes and challenges! It is very important to see setbacks as challenges and not as problems. I wanted to win Olympic gold. But there were many other athletes, from all around the world, with the exact same dream. I took that as a challenge. I didn't see why it should be a problem.

MY OLYMPIC STORY

Even before what were to be my first Olympics in Seoul, in 1988, I was running. Not from something. For something.

I managed to make the British team and there was a good chance I might win a medal. Possibly a bronze in the 400m and maybe a second of some colour in the relay.

As it turned out – and it would become a common theme throughout my career - I had a fair few injury problems leading up to those Olympic Games.

There were four rounds in the individual 400 - the heats, the second round, the semi-final and the final. As I was warming up for my heat, though, I snapped my Achilles tendon, totally putting paid to my Olympic debut. I had to watch someone else win gold, someone else take silver and someone else the bronze. I could do nothing more than watch my British relay teammates, without me, win their bronze in the 4 x 400. Believe me, that wasn't easy. For the most part, my first Olympic experience wasn't a good one. You could say it was problematic. Or, rather, you could say it presented me with a challenge.

There are clear parallels with business. You can have times when you put your heart and soul into a specific goal or project, only to find yourself, through no fault of your own, sitting on the sidelines watching the rest of your team, or worse still your competitors, win without you.

But, for me, that begs a defining question. *"Do you allow it to defeat you or do you use the experience as fuel to propel you through the next chapter in your story and on to your next victory?"* I think you can guess how I answered that question between 1988 and 1992. I treated it not as a problem but as a challenge.

In early 1992, I underwent three operations on my Achilles tendons. I was still dealing with injuries just four weeks before the Barcelona Games. I wasn't in great shape and needed to have some painkilling injections in the UK before I flew out.

I remember, when I first arrived in Spain, the soreness in my tendons meant I couldn't train for the first couple of days, despite the Team GB doctors moving heaven and earth to relieve the pain and swelling. One particular physio, Mike Garnston, worked on me around the clock. He kept me pain free and, essentially, enabled me to get back into training. He had studied my injury and taken it upon himself to learn a special technique, strapping my ankle in such a way as to take the pressure off my Achilles tendons. Before I could run when I needed to, sometimes twice a day, he took the best part of an hour to fix me up. And he did this every day without fail so I could run without pain and avoid aggravating the injury any further. He had to cut and apply the tape in special ways, layering it over and over again. It wasn't easy for him but he took the time to do it every day, whether I was training or competing. And I will never forget his help.

Nonetheless, my confidence was at an all-time low at this point. I will admit to thinking about giving up and going home because I did not want to go through what I had in Seoul four years earlier. But those thoughts didn't last long. There was no chance I was going to give up on my dream – one I had now spent 8 years striving for.

My mind jumped back to something that happened to me in the Team GB training camp in Tokyo just before the 1988 Games. I was (as always) waiting to be seen in the physio room. There were perhaps two weeks to go before the Games started and I was struggling with, you guessed it, my Achilles tendons.

The Americans were training at the same facility as us and I was approached by one of their team members, herself a 400m runner. She looked at me and asked if I was OK. I was feeling pretty sorry for myself and told her I'd had enough of all of this and was just going to give up and go home. She then gave me a piece of advice that has stuck with me to this very day. She told me that, if I was to give up just two weeks before the Games began, I would never know if I could, or would, have made it to the start line or even to win a medal. Instead, I would always live my life wondering. But, if I did everything I possibly could between now and the race, and it didn't work out, at least I would know I gave it my all. Even if it didn't work out the way I wanted. It was great advice and I took it. As I sit here writing this, I know many, many years later that there was nothing more that could have been done to get me out on the track back in 1988. And you know what? I can live with that. But I couldn't have lived with never knowing, so thank you, Denean Howard-Hill, for those wise words.

So, back to 1992. As I started my final month's training, things started off steady. In the beginning I felt very sluggish and heavy. My legs were not turning over the way I wanted them to and I was not running anywhere near as quickly as I needed to or was capable of.

A sprinter would never want to be in that position during the close season, let alone a month out from the biggest sporting event in the world. However, once a few days of training had passed, we all began to notice I was getting better and better each day. After the first two weeks, it was all going to plan but I still remember having that voice in my head saying *"It's not going to work! Go home."* But I didn't.

I stuck with it and eventually things got better to the point where, 10 days out from my first individual 400m race, I was running very quickly. And recording some very fast times. In fact, I was smashing all my previous personal bests. As my first race approached, I began to go through the things I usually did as part of my preparations leading up to a major competition. I started planning what food was I going to eat the day before my race, what time I would go to sleep the night before, what time I would wake up and what time I would warm up. The devil is in the detail. As part of that process, five days before the first round, I ran a time trial over 300m. It's an odd distance, I know, but my coach always had me run it in a way that he referred to as a 'dress rehearsal'.

It was also a great way to measure how fast I was running, as we had the luxury of electronic timing, and to see how my Achilles would hold up under race conditions. Anyway, I ran a very quick time and it finally showed me I was in great shape. We felt that, if I could hold that form, I would definitely be in the mix for a medal. And, who knows, possibly the gold.

FINISHING MY RACE

In the first round, I was the fastest qualifier with a time of 45.03 seconds, it felt very comfortable and, as intended, I ran well within myself.

The plan had been to run somewhere around 45.5 seconds, as we thought this would be more than quick enough to win the heat. We didn't expect the clock to stop at 45.03 but it just confirmed how good a shape I was in.

My coach felt I didn't need to do any more the following day in the second round to qualify again. So, the next day, I ran to exactly the same pace and plan and recorded an almost identical time – 45.02.

It was enough to win the second round but, again, I had run well within myself. The more energy you can save, the better. And I knew I had plenty more gas in the tank for the semis and the final.

At this point, the pundits felt there were only three or four with a chance of winning gold. Fortunately, I was one of them but, the night before my semi, my Dad, my coach and I agreed that I really needed to run a full and proper race this time because it was going to take more to qualify for the final. And to qualify well.

I went through the usual procedure. The right food, the right sleep and all the rest. I woke up in the morning and ate a good breakfast, had a massage and warmed up thoroughly.

It was all going to plan and I was feeling good about a third win in three days. There was no reason I couldn't win the race, even though I did not need to as the first 4 would qualify for the final. At that level, you can't go into a race hoping you win. You must go in expecting to. You need the same mindset in business. You can't go into things hoping they work out. You have to expect them to and do everything in your power to make it happen. There is no such thing as a free victory in sport. Or in business.

I can still remember hearing the gun as if it was yesterday. I had a great start in lane five. The fastest out of the blocks. For those of you who don't know how staggered lanes in a 400m race work, it might seem like the athlete in the outside lane, number eight, has an advantage because they're further round the bend at the start. But, by the time you have run both bends, the stagger has equaled out and everyone runs the same distance. That means from lane five you can see everyone in the lanes outside you but you can not really tell where the people on the inside of you are.

Nonetheless, after 100m I knew I was going well. As I turned into the back straight, I could see I was catching the guys on my outside and that there wasn't anybody catching me on the inside. Then, at the 150m mark, I heard a funny noise. A loud pop. You really don't hear the crowd when your competing. You don't hear all the yelling around you. You might hear the overall buzz but you don't hear any one person or one particular sound. All you really hear is your breath and your footsteps.

First hearing the pop, I thought it was something in the crowd. And certainly not my hamstring. So, I said to myself, *"C'mon, Derek concentrate!"* and continued haring down the back straight. Now, hamstring injuries are, unfortunately, pretty common in athletics. A sprinter pulling a hamstring is a bit like a cyclist getting a puncture. It's not a question of whether you are going to pull one, more a question of when and where it happens. And how big an impact it has. I am glad to say, though, that the medical side of the sport has moved on. Although athletes still pull hamstrings, it doesn't now occur as often as it did during my time.

As I refocused and continued to run, I suddenly felt intense pain in the back of my leg. It was like being stabbed or shot. I grabbed my leg just as it became obvious what had just happened. It was a hamstring pull. And a bad one at that. When you pull a hamstring in full flight, the only thing you want to do is stop right there. Every stride is agony, to put it mildly, so that's what I tried to do. But halting your momentum at that speed means pretty much one thing only. You go down. Hard. I was supposed to be running the most important race of my life. But instead I'm on the ground, injured yet again, slapping the track and turning the air blue. There were almost 75,000 people in the stadium, all watching the big race unfold. And there's me, on the deck, beside myself with frustration.

A few seconds passed. I was still in a lot of pain and very upset. And I couldn't escape the question – WHY ME?

But, all of a sudden, I remembered where I was. This was the Olympic semi-final. Somewhere I'd dreamt of being for so long. Dreamt of acing.

I sat up and looked around to see the other athletes were about 120m from the finish line. And that's when I had a crazy thought. If I got up right now, I could still catch them and qualify!

The first 4 athletes across the line would make the the final. In my mind, I could still be one of them. So, I got up and started running. But really, I was just hobbling. By the time I got to the 200m mark, I looked across again only to see everyone had already finished.

The race was over and I was still only halfway round. I had two choices. One, to stop and give up or, two, to set myself a new goal. To finish my race. It's at times like these that the temptation might be to quit. But, equally, that's when our mental training kicks in. I remembered exactly where I was. It was the Olympic semi-final and I said to myself *"I'm going to finish this race, even if it's the last race I ever run."* (Which incidentally it did turn out to be.) Four years previously at the 1988 Seoul Olympics, I never even made it onto the track after sustaining an injury in the warm-up for the first round. This time was different. I was going to finish my race. I was not going to be defeated by the Olympics again.

Even if it meant I would finish last, at least I was going to finish. I could live with finishing last but I couldn't live with not finishing at all. That was the reason I kept going. I had to.

It's much the same in business. We are always faced with challenges. So, you just have to rise to them. No matter how serious or how difficult they might seem, they're defining moments in our lives. They can break you and your business or they can make you and your business. But, if you do not try to overcome them, you will never know! Do you remember the advice I was given back in 1988 by the American athlete Denean Howard?

As I sit here now, some 25 years later, I know it was the right thing for me to do. I could never have lived with myself, if I hadn't got up, dusted myself down and finished what I had started.

A CHAMPION IN EVERYONE
ELSE'S EYES

There were people all around me trying to get me off the track, so the second semi-final could get under way. Put me on a stretcher or shove me in a wheelchair, just to get me out of the way. But I wasn't having any of it. I was focused on that one thing. Finishing my race. Because, when you boil it all down, the real secret to never giving up lies in how well we can focus on what we can control. In my case and in that moment, I could control my ability to finish.

I remember, as I was just about to enter the home straight with about 100m to go, a figure appeared over my left shoulder. I thought they were going to try to manhandle me off the track, so I was ready to defend myself. I was going to finish no matter what. But then I heard a familiar voice. *"Derek,*

29

it's me. You don't have to do this!"

I realised it was my Dad. Somehow, he'd made it out of his seat, through the stands, past the armed security guards, and on to the track. And he was right there beside me. He said again, *"You don't have to do this!"* But I said, *"Yes, I do!"*

I was still angry. Still swearing. I told him, come hell or high water, I was going to finish this race. He needed to get me back in lane five. It was the first and the last time I've ever been able to swear at my Dad and get away with it. He said to me, *"Okay. If you're going to finish this race, we'll finish it together."* Dad put his arm around me. And together we struggled back into lane five and on towards the line. My Dad was as strong as an ox that day. I had totally lost it emotionally. I couldn't believe it. Here I was in the Olympic Games and it was happening to me again. Why me?

I heard my Dad's voice telling me I was a champion in everybody else's eyes but I wasn't really listening to what he was saying. Neither could I really hear the reaction of the crowd. I didn't hear the thunderous applause of 75,000 people, as we crossed the finish line. It wasn't until later, when I watched the replay back, that I realised everyone was cheering me on.

As we crossed the line, I remember looking up and seeing me listed on the scoreboard in 8th place. With the letters 'DISQ' next to my name. I was disqualified for receiving outside help. But I still felt I'd finished my race. I could live with finishing last and even with being disqualified but I could not live with not having finished my race. That was when I began to learn that most important of lessons. Never give up. Finish your race. And that became the fuel for everything I do in life, whether it's in the sporting or the business arena.

THE NEXT CHALLENGE

All I wanted to do was get out of Barcelona and back home as soon as I humanly could. I didn't want to be around athletes or athletics and the last thing I wanted to watch was the Olympic 400m final.

In less than 48 hours, I was on a plane and an operation had been scheduled to get my hamstring sorted. I wanted to get home and get my leg fixed up because I had come up with a new plan. A new goal, a new target for 1992.

There was another competition at the end of the year, the IAAF World Cup in Cuba and I had my new objective. Making the GB team. I would regain my fitness, win my spot on the team, go to the World Cup and win it. I was going to prove that I could have won the Olympic 400m title.

After rest following the operation on my hamstring, I was ready and began light training again. But after just a few days' training, pop! The hamstring went again, ending any hopes of me competing in that World Cup, or indeed at all again in 1992. So, it was back into hospital and another op. This time I took a lot more time recovering. But, when I eventually resumed training, I soon heard the now familiar pop.

This went on and on. By 1994, I had pulled the same hamstring seven times and had seven operations in just 18 months. I received a call from my surgeon, asking if I would go and see him. I did as requested, going with my Dad and my coach, and I remember it like yesterday. The long and short of it was that my hamstring would not withstand the pressure of training and that my career as a professional athlete was over.

"You are never going to compete for your country again. You may as well go and get a proper job." Blunt. And painful.

I remember thinking to myself "Get off that fence, doc. Just say it like it is!" But the strange thing was, on the way to see him, I'd had a pretty good idea what he was going to say.

To be honest, his message was no great surprise but the words *'never going to compete for your country again'* stuck with me. I couldn't get them out of my head. They were like a knife to my heart and I could hear his pompous voice saying them over and over. But the idea I held on to more than anything was *"never give up."* The 1994 season was fast approaching and the last place I wanted to be was in the UK watching a load of athletics I couldn't take part in. So, I decided to go to The States, stay with a good friend of mine and keep myself in as good shape as possible. I wanted to forget what was happening back home.

For obvious reasons, I couldn't run at anything like my usual level but I kept myself fit with endless circuits, swimming pool work and a little bit of running. I certainly wasn't sprinting as quickly as before but I did manage to play a lot of basketball.

I was a big basketball fan and, as we all know, it's huge in America. There are nets everywhere, so I just played. About three hours a day. It was fine on the hamstring because I wasn't running flat out. It turned out that spending a few months training and hiding away from the world of athletics was just what the doctor ordered. And, with all of that, I discovered a new focus, a new goal and I was determined to be strong.

In business, there will be setbacks. Make no mistake about it. Sometimes, the goals you reach will be different to the ones you originally set. And, sometimes, you won't reach your goal at all because you can't control all the determining factors. But, what you can control is persevering. Not giving up and finding the fuel you need to propel yourself toward your objective.

There are very few businesspeople or entrepreneurs who make it successfully on their first attempt. Many of the most successful people fail before they succeed. In many cases, more than once. In sport we learn so much from setbacks. Losing a race or an injury. It's exactly the same in business. So, we must use setbacks and even failures as lessons and learn from them. As my Dad always told me, there is nothing wrong with making mistakes. But making the same mistakes over and over again is a real problem.

With my time up in the US, I finally headed back to the UK. I had no idea what I was going to do with the rest of my life as my athletic career was now over.

But I loved playing basketball and I decided to join a local team close to where I lived. It was just a small team and we played after work. I wasn't being paid and I did it just for fun but it was something for me to focus on. I played for them all season and we ended up winning our local league and the local cup final. It was great and, importantly, I was competing again. After the cup final, I remember we were celebrating in the changing room, when in walked a coach from the Birmingham Bullets. He asked me to come and try out for them. I had no hesitation and made the team for the following season. I was now back in professional sport, just where I wanted to be. And it got better.

Part way through the season, I was asked to try out for the England Basketball team and to play in a one-off game. Again, I went to the trials, made the team. and before I knew it, I was picked to compete for my country again.

Game day arrives. I'm on the bench for the first two quarters but I didn't mind one bit. I was loving the occasion and the atmosphere, and I knew it was only a matter of time before the coach pointed to me. In the third quarter, we were sixty points up when the coach tells me to strip off. He is going to put me on. I jump up, I tear off my tracksuit top and I'm on. I am representing my country again. The stuff dreams are made of.

We won the game and, as always, there were celebrations after the final buzzer. The crowd were on their feet, music was pumping, photographers were snapping away. It was magic. And one of the photographers recognised me from my athletics days. We had a quick chat and I asked him if he would send some photos of me playing that day.

True to his word, he sent me a handful of shots of me playing. When the envelope dropped through my letterbox, I ripped it open and started flicking through the photos. I took the best one and did what all good sportspeople do. I put it in a frame and hung it on the wall. But then I stood back and looked at it for a few seconds and came to a decision. I was going to send this photo to someone I knew. Someone who had played a very important role in me eventually making that basketball team. I took it off the wall, out of its frame and signed it. And sent it to my surgeon. The one who told me I would never compete for my country again. I wrote, *"Thanks for the vote of confidence, Doc. Signed Derek Redmond, International athlete AND International basketball player."*

So, there's something that can motivate you to achieve your goal. Something to give us the fuel we need. I always tell people to use whatever motivation they can to succeed. There are always people out there who want to see you fail. Or who believe you are incapable of attaining your goals. What greater motivation can you get? It's rocket fuel. Use it. Back to the story. Having faced down my hamstrings and having played for my country in a second sport, I knew I was ready for my next challenge.

A few Brits had competed for their country in two but not one of them had ever done it in three. I was going to try to be that guy and I chose rugby to bring it to pass. I'd played it to a good level in my schooldays and thought that, with some real hard work, I might, just might, get a call-up.

I worked my butt off playing for a local team, which bore fruit when I was asked to play professionally at Coventry RFC. I knew being picked for the full 15 a-side England team would be a tough ask but I did think there was an outside chance if I focused my efforts on Rugby Sevens.

So, I gave it everything, devoting 7 or 8 years to my new objective. I never quite made it to international level but it certainly wasn't for the lack of trying. I had already learnt, in all those years in other sports was that, if you really want something, do not let anything get in your way. I would learnt that too many people give up mentally on a dream long before it becomes a physical impossibility. Far too many of us throw in the towel way too early on our goals.

It might be something totally out of our control. There may be nothing you can ultimately do to achieve your goal. But never stop until you are stopped. Even then, if you can hobble through, finish what you start. Finish your race.

ACCEPTING CHANGE

After so many great years in professional sport and with the fact I wasn't getting any younger, I needed to look at the next chapter of my life. I needed to think about what I was going to do with the rest of my life.

What was I going to do for work? How could I put what I had learnt over the last 20 years to the best use over the next 20 years and more?

I started my own company as a personal trainer. I had spent so many years training during my career and I'd had a fantastic strength and conditioning coach, Mike Pratt. He had not only coached me well but taught me an enormous amount, so I had a lot to give. And it went well but I wanted more. I wanted to set myself a bigger challenge in the business world. Why not? If I could make a success of myself in sport, there was no reason I couldn't replicate it in the business arena. For me, it really does come down to your attitude and your mindset. So, I decided to tackle the corporate world with the same attitude I'd attacked sport.

Mike and I set up a company that made gym and fitness equipment. Despite us being relative rookies, it grew very quickly. We were happy with our success but, alas, it didn't last too long. Beset by financial problems, the company went down. As quickly as it had risen in the early days.

We lost a lot of money. We made a lot of mistakes. But I learned a lot from the experience. And I never let it break my sprit or upset my dreams of success. In sports, you have to be as strong mentally as you are physically. Mentally strong people, whether in sport or business, don't go around feeling sorry for themselves or the circumstances they find themselves in. They don't dwell on what might have been.

We learn to take responsibility for our actions and their consequences. We understand life isn't always fair. And we know that, at times, we have to be thankful for the lessons adversity can teach us. And emerge wiser and stronger.

After the gym equipment debacle, I started doing a little bit of motivational speaking. I shared the story of what had happened to me in both sport and business. I passed on how I'd found that successful sportspeople share many of the same qualities as successful businesspeople. From my first speaking gig back in 1997, my simple message of never giving up and finishing your race began to resonate. I had more and more requests and things grew to where I find myself today.

I am frequently asked how I transitioned from the world of sport to the world of business and how I managed change. I explain that change isn't necessarily a bad thing. It can be very good. And it is always worth embracing.

Back in 1991, I was competing at the World Championships Tokyo. I was in my usual two events. The individual 400m and the 4 x 400m relay. And it's the relay I want to concentrate on here. Our relay team was without doubt already world-class. We were expected to finish in the medals. Most people predicted we'd win a silver medal, behind the US. They were favourites for very good reason. They were the reigning World and Olympic champions, the world record holders and had the fastest time in the world that year. And, if that wasn't enough, the Americans hadn't been defeated in a

Men's 4 x 400m relay final at World or Olympic level for well over 50 years.

We were very good but the odds were stacked pretty high against us. As the World Championships progressed in Tokyo, I was questioning my physical ability again. I hadn't run as well as hoped in the individual event and I suggested to both my personal coach and the relay coach that maybe I should pull out of the relay. I really didn't want to let the rest of the team down and felt the other five guys in the team would do fine without me.

But my coach was adamant I had what it takes to run and to run well, and it was decided that I would compete in the heats. We would then make a decision on whether I was fit and fast enough to take my place in the final. So, for the heats, the coaches went with Kriss Akabusi, Mark Richardson, Ade

48

Mafe and myself. It was a strong team and we won our heat, qualifying faster than everyone else, including the Americans, who we shaded on the stopwatch. And, like us, they had strength in depth, with a couple of rapid guys to draft in for the final.

After our heat, I had a bit of a performance debrief with both coaches. I felt I was quick enough to run in the final, as did they, so the relay coach told the squad his selection and the order in which he wanted us to run. Now, the order – who passes the baton to who - is important in a 4 x 400m relay.

Conventional thinking says the fastest of the four brings it home and the second quickest goes from the gun. The other two guys take the second and third legs.

Our coaches went with tradition, putting me on the first leg and Kriss Akabusi on the second, followed by John Regis and finally Roger Black, who had just won a silver medal in the individual 400m – on form, the quickest guy and the one to go for it on the final lap.

The night before the race, we ate properly and retired to our rooms. John Regis and I were sharing, so we settled down for the night. At around 10pm, there was knock at the door. Kriss and Roger wanted to discuss the order. They were convinced that, if we changed the order, we could win. The idea was that, instead of deploying our quickest guy, Roger, on the last leg, we should use Kriss. The logic? Kriss believed he was in the form of his life. Not only had he just won bronze in the 400m hurdles, but he'd done it despite misjudging his race. He was certain, had he executed that race better, taking gold was well within his capabilities.

Roger, who we'd normally expect to surge ahead of Kriss in training, backed him to the hilt. He'd seen how hard Kriss had been pushing him in our sessions. He felt he was strong enough to chase down the Americans on the final leg, if he was close enough with 40 metres to go. So, the plan, as we saw it, was so - if we could hand Kriss the baton, with a deficit of five metres or fewer to the Americans, he would run down the guy likely to take their final leg, Antonio Pettigrew, the newly crowned World 400m champion. Roger would use his pace from the off, hand over to me on the second leg and then we would give big John the task of

setting up Kriss for a monster fourth leg. It made a lot of sense but, at the same time, it was a risk and we would need the buy-in of the coaches to go ahead. They had the final say. To convince them to make such a leap faith would take some doing. But convince them we did. We were clear a change of this kind, but unconventional, would give us the best chance of taking gold from the Americans. The new order was this – Roger to me, me to John and John to Kriss. Hopefully, with little to no gap for him to make up on the US athlete. Quite the gamble.

The next evening, Roger myself and John put in three great legs and managed to hand Kriss that baton less than a metre behind Pettigrew for that all-important final leg. With 80 metres to go, Kriss made his move. We cheered him on as he passed Pettigrew 30 metres from the line and held on to the tape. We had won. It was the very first time anyone had overpowered an American 4 x 400m relay team at World or Olympic level for 57 years. To do so, we'd made a very big change. We went against the grain. We swam against the tide. And we pulled it off. We were the 1991 IAAF 4 x 400m World champions. And it felt unbelievable!

Going back to the subject of change, that story from Tokyo in 1991 just goes to show how change can be very much for the good. So, if change can make a difference to your business or to your career, welcome it. Embrace it. Your biggest fear should not be of the unknown. The threats of stagnation or complacency are far greater. Success is a process. You move from one state to another. The absence of success to the presence of success. That is change in itself.

So, becoming successful is a story of change. It requires change. And, in change, there's always room for uncertainty. Nothing is guaranteed. But that uncertainty can bring out the best in you, just as it did with us back in 1991. So, don't be afraid of change. Don't waste energy on things beyond your control. In 'bad' or 'difficult' situations, recognise that you can always control your own response and your own attitude. And, if you respond positively and adopt the right attitude, you can accomplish anything.

Be prepared to take risks. Not dumb and dangerous ones, of course, but calculated, considered risks. Weigh up the risks, the potential downsides and even the worst case scenarios. Do it thoroughly and you will, more often than not, work through the challenges. That is what they are. Challenges. Do not look at them as problems. The Tokyo story is also informative in another way. We couldn't have achieved what we did without one vital ingredient. Let's tackle the subject of teamwork. One of the subjects I am asked to speak about most frequently.

It played a very important part in us becoming world champions. People often ask me how did our team defeat the Americans?

You have to remember all four Americans were faster than all of us on paper. In fact, if you take personal bests into account, they had a three second advantage over us.

That equates to around 27 metres on the track, so the question is perfectly valid. How did we win that race? Well, it took a lot of hard work in the background but the simple answer is that it came down to great teamwork. But what does that really mean. For me, great teams need great individuals. But that's not the whole story. You need something extra. One of the great things about our 1991 World title team of six - including Ade Mafe and Mark Richardson, who didn't run in the final – was how well we gelled as a team. But consider this.

A relay team is made up of the six best 400m runners in the country. Or, to put it another way, the top six 400m *rivals* in the country. So, basically, we were six guys who all wanted to be the 400 metre Number One 400m athlete. Not just in the UK but in the world. We spent the majority of our time training to beat each other.

It was only in short bursts around major championships that we were expected to come together as a team, and train and work together for the common good. Kind of counter-intuitive, given the underlying rivalries. To overcome them, we spent several weekends training together as a squad. Not just on physical aspects, to be honest, but more for the mental side of things.

Getting to know each other, understanding each other's motivators and demotivators. What to say and what not to say to each other. By the time we got to Tokyo, we knew each other really well. So well, in fact, that some 27 years later we are all still very close friends. We still spend time in each other's company, mainly hacking our way around the golf course. Despite the fact we were some-time rivals, we forged close bonds of friendship. We knew it would maximise our chances of success. We had fantastic communication. We were not afraid to have honest conversations, when necessary. And we had total trust and faith in each other. For me, that's vital to a winning team. We weren't afraid to try something new. In our case, changing the order in which we ran. You may ask if it matters which order you run but it really does. Even though every leg is 400m, they are all different in the way that you run them. Having the right person on the right leg is vital.

The original order set by our coaches was the obvious, conventional one. And, by any 'normal' measure, probably the correct one. But, after all six team members had had their say, we felt the only way we were going to win gold was to make a change. Our proposed new order had never been tried before. While we knew it was the winning order, it was just a theory with no supporting test data, so to speak. And, the night before the biggest 4 x 400m race in years, we were faced with the task of talking our coaches into it. As a team, though, we were all behind the plan and fully prepared to live with the consequences.

Nothing was going to stop us running in that order. With the courage of our convictions, nothing was going to stop us achieving our objective. I like to think of a team as being a bit like a wheel. It has a hub and number of spokes. Now, thinking of your place in your business, imagine yourself as the hub. Draw in your mind a spoke for each member of your team. In my case, in 1991, there were five but it doesn't matter how many, just as long as you have one for each member. Then draw a circle around them to complete your wheel. Putting yourself in the wheel's middle is key. In no way does it mean you're the most important person in the team. Think of it more in terms of your connectedness with every other individual.

You interact with them all and your actions induce some sort of reaction in each person. And subsequently on the whole team and the outcomes you're aiming to bring about.

If you keep that dynamic in your thoughts and take care of your responsibilities to the team and to your colleagues, you can become one of the great individuals every great team needs.

RELEASING THE CONTROL

I learned another great lesson during my sporting career and carried it through into business.

I understood that I should never waste time or energy worrying about things over which I have no control. And I must thank my sports psychologist, Brian Millar, for opening my eyes on the subject.

He taught me to stay focused on my goals and put 100% effort into the areas I could command. And he set it all out on paper in a simple triangle divided horizontally in three. Top, middle and bottom sections.

In the top section of the triangle you write your goal, your dream, your outcome. Mine was to win an Olympic gold medal. Yours could well be something entirely different. The first thing to understand is that you have no control over whether you achieve your outcome. I couldn't control whether or not I won that Olympic gold, as I couldn't stop someone else running quicker than me in any given race. It may sound defeatist but it's totally realistic. Someone else could be a supreme talent. I might fall ill on the big day. You get the picture.

The variables, when you really think about them are almost endless. And I have no control over them.

Next, in the middle of the triangle, write down the actions you have identified as necessary to take in order to achieve the goal at the top of your triangle. Looking at my example again, I knew that, if I could record a time of 43 seconds dead in an Olympic final, there was a very strong possibility that would be more than sufficient to top the podium and I have an element of control over achieving that. If my times in training were suggesting I was on course to run 43 seconds, if my coach, Tony Hadley, and I had planned my peak for that Olympic final correctly, and if I executed the race as planned, then I had some control. That sounds like a lot of ifs. But I can influence all of those variables.

Now look to the bottom section of the triangle. It so happens to be the biggest. Write down all the actions you need to complete in order to achieve what you have written in the middle section of the triangle. In my case, that was things like my diet, my sleep, my weight training, my track work. In fact, all elements of my training and preparation. I have total control over all these actions. I could choose the food I ate. I could determine when and how much sleep and rest I had. I was the one who could take myself down to the track or the gym and make sure I put in the necessary work during in each and every session. It is at this section that you should direct all your time and effort. You have total control.

We mentioned that the bottom section is the biggest of the three. If you focus on it, it will deliver the biggest impact. Breaking your goal down into manageable chunks or items on an agenda, you can do what needs to be done to achieve your objective. I refer to this section of the triangle as 'taking care of business'. So, don't think about or focus too much on the bit at the top. If you 'take care of business', see to the things you can control at the base of the triangle, then you are maximizing your chances of achieving the things you can influence in the middle section. If you can tick those middle section boxes, you have a fantastic opportunity to achieve the goal at the apex. Your ultimate ambition. I couldn't control what other people around me were doing, so I released that control. I didn't worry about it and I didn't expend unnecessary energy trying to control the uncontrollable. So, when we relinquish control over the thing we aim to achieve most, when we learn to complete the tasks we can control, we put ourselves in a great position to fulfill our dreams.

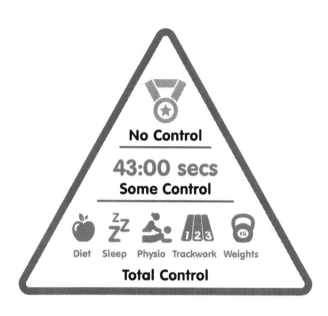

No Control

43:00 secs
Some Control

Diet   Sleep   Physio   Trackwork   Weights

Total Control

CHALLENGES NOT PROBLEMS

Keep in mind that, no matter how successful you are, things can and do go wrong. When they do, you can choose to look at them as problems or to see them as challenges to overcome and lessons from which to learn.

The lesson I took from my Barcelona experience was that I could choose to turn things into whatever I wanted them to be. All I did in that Olympic semi-final was pull a hamstring. That's nothing in comparison to some of the challenges others have faced and defeated.

So, I chose to see that setback as a challenge rather than as a problem. Sticking to the same logic, I could face a lifetime of challenges but, equally, I could find ways to surmount them. There are people who see life as problematic. They see the bad in a situation and, surprise, surprise, they end up with a bad outcome.

By the same token, there are people who take the positives out of life. Guess what their outcomes tend to look like. I am privileged to know and to have worked with Naomi Riches, a young Paralympic champion rower. Her eyesight is, sadly, severely impaired. And, throughout her early life, people were always telling her she couldn't do this or couldn't do that because of it.

They used her sight as the reason she wouldn't succeed. As a limit to her potential. Knowing no different, she bought the negativity until somebody changed her thinking. They told her *"you are obviously a very talented rower and, because of your sight, I think you could, one day, become a Paralympic champion."*

So, she worked very hard, she controlled the things she could control and, in 2008, won a bronze medal at her first Paralympics.

What's more, four years later in 2012 in front of her home crowd in London, she took gold. Prophecy turned to reality. The absence of success turned into the presence of success.

She was a Paralympic champion. Because she opened herself to possibilities instead of closing herself off with limitations. Naomi is just one of scores of examples I know of people who choose to accept things as challenges rather than see them as problems. And I bet you too could name several people in your life who do exactly that. Draw strength from them. Listen to them. Find out just what it is that makes them keep on pushing forward. Driving themselves onward to success rather than give up at the first, second or even third hurdle.

I sometimes like to think of life as a bit like a Rubik's cube. It can be relatively simple to complete one side, to make all the squares the same colour. That's great. You begin to see the fruit of your labour quite quickly and you're spurred with your job. Or, in this case, your cube.

But, just as in life, the further you progress, the harder it can get. As you get closer and closer to completing all six sides, it gets more difficult. You persevere until there are just a few squares still in the wrong place. That's when it's important to learn to look at the problem and turn it into a challenge. It can be frustrating to get that far yet fail to finish the cube. Having spent many years playing with Rubik's cubes, I have found that, every time I reach this critical point, I must think of it not as a problem. Just as another challenge to overcome. Then, I break it down, work it out, complete the cube and reach my goal.

Yes. Those last few squares can take as long to as the rest of the cube. You might think you're going backwards, messing up the cube, rather than getting closer to solving the damn thing. But, when you finally nail it, the satisfaction is immense.

It's no different in life or business. Sometimes we seem to be putting so much effort into something when we feel we're no closer to our goal. But if we push through it, qualities like discipline, self-belief, confidence and stubbornness can really pay dividends.

FIVE STEPS TO SUCCESS

I remember once presenting at a secondary school. The subject of success came up in a Question & Answer session. A student put up his hand and asked me a simple but great question. *"What were my five simple steps to success?"* He wanted a simple plan to follow.

I didn't, at first, think I could boil it down to five simple steps. But, after giving it a little thought, I gave him his answer. And, the more I thought about it, the more I understood that my five simple steps could work for anyone.

Step 1 – Set a Goal

Success means different things to different people. It does not matter what your goal or dream may be. You might want to be the next president, sportsperson, a rock star, a doctor or whatever. But, if you don't know where you want to go, how do you know where you are on the path or and when you've finally arrived? It's like a car journey. You may have the first few roads planned but you have no idea what's going to happen further along the way or how many people are coming with you.

With no destination do you just drive around until you run out of fuel?

It sounds crazy but that's what millions of us do. We want to be successful in an abstract way. But we have no idea how we want to be successful. So, it all starts when we set ourselves a goal. An objective. An end-state. A destination.

Step 2 - Commit to Your Goal

After you have set that goal, you must commit to it. If your goal is to lose weight and you continue to eat doughnuts, that's not commitment. When you actually stop eating doughnuts - something you really enjoy – you have committed.

Commitment is a great confidence booster. Every time you resist a doughnut craving, you show more and more drive towards your weight loss goal. I can remember hundreds of times really not wanting to get up out of my warm bed at 6am and go out in the cold to train.

But, you know what? I did get up. I was glad I got up. And the fact that I had meant I could drag myself out again and again and again.

As many times as I had to…

Step 3 – Motivation

Motivation is key. But finding a source of motivation can be difficult. So, you might try a technique that served me well while I was running.

I used to do it a lot. I used to write the names and personal bests of the top ten athletes in the world in my event on little postcards. I would then write my own name and time in red, whether I was in that top ten or not, and stick them everywhere - on the bathroom mirror, on the inside of my front door, on the sun visor of my car, on my fridge — you get the picture.

Wherever I went, I would see their names and times. If I'm totally honest, I got sick of seeing them after a while. But it helped me immensely. I wanted my name at the top of the list. Not hidden somewhere in the middle. Or worse still at the bottom. And, constantly reminded of the guys who were faster than me, I'd go to the track and train like a man possessed.

Step 4 - Teamwork

We can't always achieve our goals on our own. Often, we need help from others and there's no shame in asking for it. When I'm talking to students, for example, I always tell them there's no shame in talking to their mums, dads, brothers and sisters. Peers at school or even the teachers. If they can help you, they will.

If people see you working and striving for your goal, and they see you've made the commitment and that you're motivated, you'll be surprised how many people will help you. They can see the desire in you. And they want to be a part of your success.

Step 5 – Self-belief

This is the most important step, certainly for

young people. Believe you can achieve your goals. It's that simple. Have faith in your abilities. If you don't believe in yourself, how can you expect anybody else to believe in you?

SUCCESS IN LIFE AND IN BUSINESS

You can reach your goals, no matter what success actually looks like to you. You can reach your goals in life and in business. But, for it to happen, you must start by setting those goals.

You must lay down a marker and set out what it's going to take to achieve it.

Then focus your attention on the daily actions you can take to make it happen. In the end, it's not about whether or not you become a gold medalist.

It's about taking care of business. Dealing with the things you can control en route to – hopefully - becoming a gold medalist.

Rather than comparing yourself with the people around you, you should simply work out your destination and then work out the key milestones on the journey. And, in that, you will find your own formula for success.

Focus. Set those goals. Use and learn from the challenges along the way. Find the fuel you need to succeed and never give up. If you do those things well, you will then be the champion of your life and in your business.

I encourage you to reach for your idea of success. It's there for you in all the small things you do. They add up to something much greater than the sum of their parts. So, never give up and finish your race.

Printed in Poland
by Amazon Fulfillment
Poland Sp. z o.o., Wrocław

54423111R00047